W9-BKC-667

Robert Fulton

Innovator with Steam Power

Peggy J. Parks

BLACKBIRCH™
PRESS

THOMSON
━━━✦━━━ ™
GALE

San Diego • Detroit • New York • San Francisco • Cleveland
New Haven, Conn. • Waterville, Maine • London • Munich

THOMSON

GALE

Photo Credits: cover, pages 5, 22, 44 © Hulon|Archive by Getty Images; pages 7, 18, 21, 43, 48, 53, 57 © Blackbirch Archive; pages 8, 58 © Lee Snider/Corbis; pages 10–11 © Len Delessio/Index Stock; pages 12, 52 © Robert Fulton/Henry Luce III Center (New-York Historical Society); pages 14–15 © Historical Picture Archive/Corbis; page 17 © The Art Archive/Dagli Orti; pages 20, 37, 50–51 © Bettmann/Corbis; page 25 © National Portrait Gallery, Smithsonian Institution/Art Resource, NY; page 26 © Michael Nicholson/Corbis; pages 28, 29 © Library of Congress; pages 30, 32–33, 38 © Mary Evans Picture Library; page 34 © The Bridgeman Art Library; page 36 © Dover; page 46 © Archivo Iconografico, S.A./Corbis; pages 54, 55 © Picture History

LIBRARY OF CONGRESS CATALOGING-IN-PUBLICATION DATA

Parks, Peggy J., 1951-
  Robert Fulton / by Peggy J. Parks.
    p. cm. — (Giants of science)
  Summary: Surveys the life and accomplishments of American inventor and
mechanic, Robert Fulton, who is best known for building the first successful steamboat.
Includes bibliographical references and index.
  ISBN 1-56711-492-X (hardback : alk. paper)
  1. Fulton, Robert, 1765–1815—Juvenile literature. 2. Marine engineers—United
States—Biography—Juvenile literature. 3. Inventors—United States—Biography—
Juvenile literature. 4. Steamboats—History—Juvenile literature. [1. Fulton, Robert, 1765-
1815. 2. Inventors. 3. Steamboats--History.] I. Title. II. Series.

VM140.F9P37 2003
623.8'24'092—dc21

                                                                    2003008048

Printed in China
10 9 8 7 6 5 4 3 2 1

CONTENTS

Voyage of the *North River* 4

Early Childhood 7

A Rebellious Spirit. 9

Young Inventor 9

An Artistic Young Man 12

New Adventures 12

Life-Threatening Illness. 13

Voyage to Europe 13

A New Life in England 16

From Artist to Inventor. 16

Focus on Canals 17

Dabbling with Steam Engines 19

A Mechanical Excavator 20

Fulton as Author. 23

Decision to Leave England 24

Paris 25

"A Curious Machine for
    Mending Politics". 26

The First Submarine 27

The Nautilus 28

A Miniature Submarine 31

From Hope to Despair. 32

The First Panorama in Paris 34

A Machine for Making Rope 36

Renewed Focus on Submarines. . . 37

Test on the Seine 39

Taking on the British. 39

The End of the Line 41

An Important Meeting. 42

Early Steamboat Experiments 42

The Partnership. 44

From Disaster to Triumph. 45

Remarkable Turn of Events 46

Back in England 47

Full Steam Ahead 49

Romantic Notions 52

Commercial Steamboat Operation. 52

Expanding the Fleet 54

Continued Fascination with
    Weaponry 55

Bittersweet Year 56

A Steam-Powered Warship 57

Winter Tragedy 58

Fulton's Legacy 59

Important Dates 60

Glossary 62

For More Information 62

Sources 63

Index. 64

Voyage of the *North River*

On August 17, 1807, a strange-looking vessel made its way slowly up the Hudson River, heading north from New York City. People stood along the riverbank and watched in awe. The thing was obviously a boat, but it was unlike any boat they had ever seen before. It was flat-bottomed, square on the sides, and very long and thin. In the center was a large copper boiler that creaked noisily, and from it towered a fifteen-foot smokestack that gushed black smoke into the air. What puzzled the people most, though, was that the vessel had two large masts, but no sails—yet it still moved without them. On each side there were enormous wooden paddlewheels that stirred up the water and splashed furiously, propelling the boat along as they turned.

The designer of the odd-looking craft was a man named Robert Fulton. He stood on the deck and proudly rode on his boat as it chugged its way along the Hudson. It pleased him to see so many people watching him, all with looks of amazement on their faces. No one had believed it would be possible to power a boat with a steam engine. The technology had been developed in Europe more than thirty years before, but because very few steam engines existed in the United States, Americans were not familiar with them.

A number of people were not only amazed, they were also afraid. The vessel was described as "a monster moving on the waters defying the winds and tide, and breathing flames and smoke."[1] Some observers even lay down and began to pray that they would be saved from the fiery monster. Alice Crary Sutcliffe, Fulton's great-granddaughter, later wrote about the fear of sailing-boat crew members who watched the bizarre-looking sailless contraption head toward them. She said some of the sailors were so frightened that they abandoned their own boats and fled into the woods to escape.

For weeks before the maiden voyage, while Fulton's boat was still being built in New York City, he had been mocked by

Opposite: *Robert Fulton triumphed where others failed when he designed the first working steam-powered boat to grace American waterways.*

4

New Yorkers. They had laughed at his notion of a steam-powered boat and they nicknamed his vessel "Fulton's Folly." Most were not aware that Fulton had already taken his boat for a test run on the river, so he knew that it would perform the way he expected. On August 17, he set out from New York City for Albany, 130 miles upriver, accompanied by a select group of people who were closest to him. A large crowd of spectators witnessed the launch. Some who noticed the fire that powered the steam engine, and the great puffs of black smoke, expected the boat to explode at any minute. Most of the people were silent at first. Then, when they saw the vessel continue on its way, many applauded and shouted their congratulations.

The trip to Albany took thirty-two hours, and the trip back to New York City took thirty hours. This was much faster than sailing ships, which typically took fifty hours or more. After Fulton returned home, elated about the success of his maiden voyage, he wrote a letter to a friend. He described his trip on the vessel that he simply called the steamboat, which he later named the *North River*. His words were smug as he described passing many "sloops and schooners" as if they were standing still. He also expressed great satisfaction at proving his doubters wrong, as he explained: "The power of propelling boats by steam is now fully proved. The morning I left New York, there were not perhaps thirty persons in the city who believed that the boat would ever move one mile an hour, or be of the least [worth], and while we were putting off from the wharf, which was crowded with spectators, I heard a number of sarcastic remarks. This is the way in which ignorant men compliment what they call philosophers and projectors."[2]

Fulton had not invented the steamboat, nor was he the first to experiment with one. He was, however, the first to design and build a steam-powered vessel that had all the right features, and that actually worked. After his historic voyage on the *North River*, people everywhere became familiar with the name Robert Fulton. His story—the story of an amazing man known for his creativity, boldness, and brilliance—begins in the small, rural area of southeastern Pennsylvania where he was born.

Fulton was born on November 14, 1765, on the farm depicted above, in Little Britain Township, Pennsylvania.

Early Childhood

Robert Fulton was born on November 14, 1765, in Little Britain Township, a community about twenty miles south of Lancaster, Pennsylvania. His parents, Robert Fulton Sr. and Mary Smith Fulton, had five children: three daughters, Elizabeth, Isabelle, and Mary; and two sons, Robert and his younger brother, Abraham. Both Robert's father and mother were immigrants from Ireland.

When the elder Robert Fulton first moved to America, he had worked in Lancaster as a tailor. After his marriage and the birth of his daughters, he and his wife sold the family home and bought a large farm on Conowingo Creek in Little Britain. Just over nine months after they moved to the farm, Robert was born.

Robert's father had never been a farmer, and he really did not know much about being one. His lack of knowledge quickly became obvious after he moved his family to the country. His

7

The Holy Trinity Church stands in Lancaster, Pennsylvania, where young Robert grew up.

inexperience with farming, combined with harsh weather conditions, made times extremely difficult. When the senior Fulton had purchased the farm, he borrowed a great deal of money. By 1772, he was heavily in debt and had no money with which to support his family. He had no choice but to sell the farm and move with his wife and children back to Lancaster, where he resumed his work as a tailor.

Two years later, the Fultons suffered a great loss when Robert Fulton Sr. unexpectedly died. At the time of his death he had very little money, so his family was left to fend for themselves. According to biographer Cynthia Owen Philip, Mary Fulton was poor, but she managed to support her children, probably with the help of her wealthy family. Philip offers a glimpse into their lives: "There were warm fires in which to roast chestnuts, books to read aloud, and the company of affectionate friends."[3] Robert was only eight years old when his father died, yet he felt a sense of responsibility for his family because he was the oldest son. For the rest of his life he would feel protective toward his mother and siblings.

A Rebellious Spirit

Robert's first years of schooling were spent at home, where his mother taught him to read and write. She then enrolled him in a school that was run by Caleb Johnson, a Quaker man who was a shopkeeper and a building contractor, as well as a schoolmaster. Johnson was very strict and had definite ideas about how students should behave. From the beginning, Robert was a challenge because he had a feisty nature and an adventurous spirit. He also did not apply himself to his studies and once told his schoolmaster: "My head is so full of original notions that there is no vacant chamber to store away the contents of dusty books."[4] When Johnson disciplined him in an effort to make him behave, Robert rebelled by saying: "Sir, I came to have something beaten into my brains, and not into my knuckles."[5] At a time when students were expected to behave without questioning authority, Robert's defiance was especially troublesome to his schoolmaster.

Young Inventor

Even though Robert was not an easy student to handle, Johnson saw him as an intelligent, creative young man. Also, he observed that Robert's curiosity sometimes led him to analyze objects and improve them. This was the case when Robert was about ten years old and showed up late for school. When Johnson asked him where he had been, Robert replied that he had been at a local shop making a better type of pencil. The pencil had been invented in Europe more than two hundred years before, but Robert decided to make one that used a metal point instead of the usual lead. He proudly showed his pencil to the schoolmaster, who agreed that it was excellent.

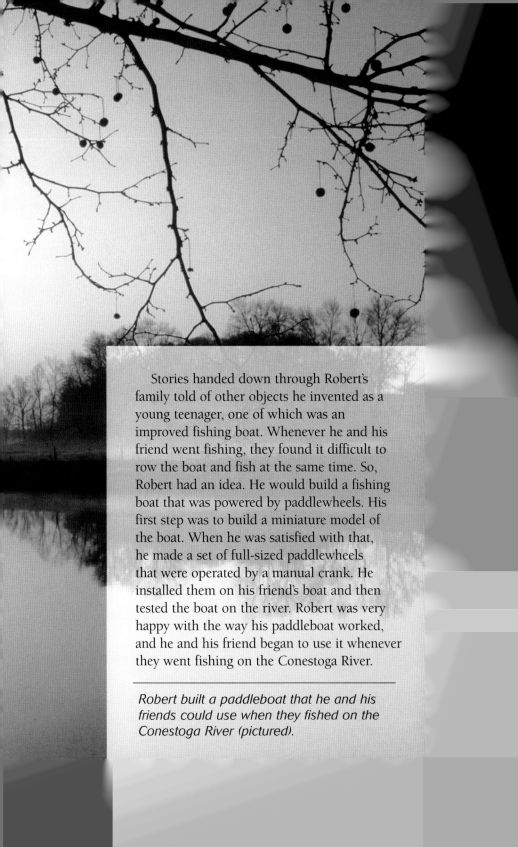

Stories handed down through Robert's family told of other objects he invented as a young teenager, one of which was an improved fishing boat. Whenever he and his friend went fishing, they found it difficult to row the boat and fish at the same time. So, Robert had an idea. He would build a fishing boat that was powered by paddlewheels. His first step was to build a miniature model of the boat. When he was satisfied with that, he made a set of full-sized paddlewheels that were operated by a manual crank. He installed them on his friend's boat and then tested the boat on the river. Robert was very happy with the way his paddleboat worked, and he and his friend began to use it whenever they went fishing on the Conestoga River.

Robert built a paddleboat that he and his friends could use when they fished on the Conestoga River (pictured).

An Artistic Young Man

Robert was said to have created other inventions during his teenage years, including household utensils for his mother and a skyrocket that he displayed during a town celebration. His family records also tell of an air gun that he designed and built, as well as other gun designs that he provided to gunsmiths in Lancaster. Because it was the time of the Revolutionary War between America and England, and there was a great demand for improved gun designs, the town's gunsmiths welcomed Robert's drawings.

From a very young age Robert was also interested in art. One day, a classmate brought a set of paints that his older brother had mixed to school. Paints were in short supply because they were usually ordered from Europe, and the war made it difficult to buy such materials. Robert was fascinated with the paints and asked to borrow them. He proved to be such a talented painter that the boy gave him the set to keep. Later, Robert used his artistic talent to paint signs for the taverns and shops throughout the town.

Robert used his artistic talent to paint miniatures like the one pictured here.

New Adventures

During his mid-teenage years, Robert decided to move to Philadelphia. His goal was not only to earn money for himself, but also to earn enough to help his family. He went to work as an apprentice for Jeremiah Andrews, a silversmith who created his own custom jewelry designs. Andrews specialized in "hair-working," an art that involved creating pieces of jewelry from human hair. During Robert's apprenticeship, he learned about jewelry making and hair-working, and he spent much of his time perfecting his painting skills.

He painted oil portraits, landscapes, and miniatures, which were tiny portraits of people. During this time, he met the prominent American statesman and inventor, Benjamin Franklin. The two eventually became friends.

Life-Threatening Illness

By 1785, Fulton was able to open his own shop, and he began to advertise himself as a painter of miniatures. He became well known in Philadelphia, and people often spoke of the intricate details and beauty of his artistic creations. Yet, even though he was a very talented artist, historians say it is likely that Fulton worked at other jobs besides painting, jewelry making, and hair-working. That is because even the most talented artists rarely made enough money from their art to support themselves and their families.

In early 1786, Fulton was stricken with a serious inflammation of the lungs, and he became very ill with a disease that was thought to be tuberculosis. In hopes of recovering from his illness, he went to stay at a well-known health resort called Warm Springs, located in Virginia. Fulton's stay at the spa did help him recover, and he returned to Philadelphia in good health. After a short time, he moved his shop to a better location in the city, where he continued his work with miniature painting and hair-working.

Voyage to Europe

During Fulton's stay at Warm Springs, he had become acquainted with some prominent people, many of whom were well-known in the world of art. They were impressed with Fulton's artistic talent and encouraged him to travel to England and study with painters who were far more skilled and esteemed than anyone in America. The idea appealed to him and he began to plan for his trip.

Fulton's first commitment, though, was to his family. His mother had long wanted to move back to the country, so in the spring of 1786, Fulton used much of his savings to buy her a farm in Washington County, Pennsylvania. He also bought parcels of land for his siblings.

In the spring of 1787 Fulton left Philadelphia for England, and he carried with him a letter of introduction written by Benjamin Franklin. The letter was addressed to Benjamin West, a highly respected American painter who had moved to England. West was a leading figure in the London art world. He was a court painter for King George III, and was also one of

The London exhibition, like the one depicted here, of Fulton's work was a success and led to paying work as a portraitist.

the founders of England's Royal Academy of Arts. He had been a tutor and sponsor for many young American men who wished to be artists, so Franklin knew he would be an excellent person for Fulton to know.

A New Life in England

Fulton arrived in London in late spring and went to visit West at his home, which was also the studio where the artist displayed his huge, dramatic paintings. West welcomed him warmly, and while it is not known whether he accepted Fulton as a pupil, he did help him find lodging at the home of another well-known painter.

The next years were difficult for Fulton because he did not earn much money. In a letter to his mother, he spoke of how hard he had to work and study to support himself while he became established as a painter. Yet even though times were hard, he did enjoy the companionship of many friends, the closest of whom was West. Fulton was a frequent visitor at West's home, and he also developed a close friendship with West's wife, Elizabeth, who affectionately called Fulton her "favorite son."

In 1791, several of Fulton's paintings were accepted by London's prestigious Royal Academy. He hoped that the exhibition would help build his credibility as an artist and lead to increased business, and it was not long before he got his wish. Lord William Courtenay, a wealthy member of England's aristocracy, invited him to visit Devonshire, England, to paint his portrait. Fulton was both delighted and honored by Courtenay's offer. He packed his personal belongings and art supplies and traveled two hundred miles to Devonshire, where he moved into Powderham Castle with Courtenay and his family. Fulton lived at the castle for a year and a half while he finished the portrait, and he later wrote that Courtenay was so pleased with the finished work that he had introduced Fulton to all of his friends. They, in turn, commissioned Fulton to paint more portraits, which earned him enough money to pay off his debts and begin to save for the future.

From Artist to Inventor

By the late 1790s, Fulton had begun to lose interest in his career as a painter. Instead, he began to focus on combining his artistic talents with his mechanical skills, as Alice Crary Sutcliffe explains: "He appears to have been reaching out in many directions of thought, to try to solve some industrial problem, great or small."[6] Fulton had become particularly fascinated with the work of local craftsmen who used different types of marble to make lovely clocks, tables, urns, and other objects. Their creations so inspired him that he developed his own machine for cutting and polishing marble. He submitted a small model of the device to London's Royal Society for the Encouragement of Arts, Manufactures, and Commerce. In 1794, the esteemed group awarded him a silver medal for the

Fulton turned his artistic energy toward the creation of a machine to cut and polish marble for tables, clocks, and other items.

invention. The inscription on the medal read, "To Mr. Robert Fulton, for his invention of a Mill for sawing Marble and other Stone, the Silver Medal. The Mill is at work near Torbay, Devon; and a Model, presented by Mr. Fulton, is reserved in the Society's Repository, for the use of the Public."[7]

Focus on Canals

Another of Fulton's inventions was something known as a double inclined plane. This was a device that could be used to raise and lower boats from one level to another in artificial waterways called canals. Fulton had become interested in canals after observing the poor transportation systems in Devonshire and Cornwall. The roads were steep, narrow, and rutted, and most goods could only be carried on the backs of ponies. In areas where river transportation was not possible, canals had already proven very useful because they allowed goods to be

17

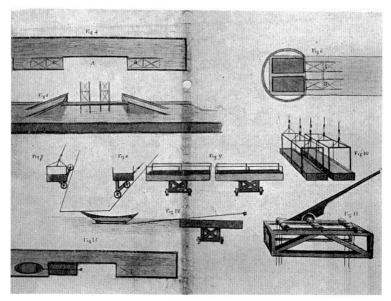

Fascinated by canals, Fulton designed the double-inclined plane, which allowed boats to move more easily through the waterways.

transported through water. Canals, however, were neither simple nor cheap to build. To construct them, deep trenches that stretched for many miles needed to be dug. Also, a system of locks required that allowed boats to pass through the canal. Locks are similar to water-filled stairs—they raise and lower water levels so boats can pass through.

Fulton later explained his enthusiasm for canal transportations: "I . . . have not painted a picture for more than two years, as I have little doubt but canals will answer my purpose much better."[8] Before he designed his double inclined plane, he spent time studying canal systems throughout England. His goal was to gain knowledge about how canals were constructed, and also to become acquainted with the people who built them.

During the 1790s, Fulton regularly corresponded with the Earl of Stanhope, one of England's most famous inventors and a leader in the field of canal building. In his first letter, Fulton presented his thoughts on canal building and described his idea for the double inclined plane. At first, Stanhope showed some interest in what Fulton had to say. He did, however, remind Fulton that the idea of an inclined-plane system was not new—others, including Stanhope himself, had devised similar lifting devices. Fulton mistook Stanhope's mild interest as a sign that he was not only excited about Fulton's work, but would perhaps even be willing to help finance it. He eagerly wrote back, offering to form a partnership with Stanhope. He was bold enough to offer his thoughts on why other inclined-plane systems—including the one devised by Stanhope—were inferior to his own. Stanhope, long known as an expert on canals, did not appreciate Fulton's remarks. He wrote to say that Fulton was not qualified to advise him about canals. The final blow was when Stanhope advised Fulton to consider a profession that was not mechanical in nature, and he also refused to provide any financial assistance for Fulton's inclined-plane system.

Fulton was discouraged by Stanhope's rejection, but it did not dampen his enthusiasm. Instead, he resolved to complete the design for his double inclined plane and win a patent for it, which would give him exclusive rights to manufacture and sell it. He prepared thirteen drawings of the system and also wrote six printed pages that described it in great detail. He used the documents to apply for his patent, which he was granted in June 1794.

> "The idea that is born in a man's mind belongs as incontestably to him as the tree that springs up in his field."
>
> —ROBERT FULTON

Dabbling with Steam Engines

Because only about sixty-five patents were issued per year, Fulton felt privileged that his was approved. He knew that the patent would give him added credibility, and he believed it would cause people to take his invention more seriously. During the summer of 1794, he decided to travel north to Manchester, which was the hub of England's canal network. A new canal was under construction there, and Fulton wanted to look at it. Not long after he arrived, he was hired by a group called the Peak Forest Company to work on the project.

James Watt, pictured in this engraving, revolutionized the steam engine but was not interested in Fulton's ideas on steam power.

For a short time during 1794, Fulton turned his interest toward steam power. From his ongoing correspondence with Stanhope he was undoubtedly aware of Stanhope's long-standing interest in steam transportation. He was also likely aware that Stanhope had designed a steam vessel called the Ambinavigator, but had been unable to get a steam engine built that could power it. In November 1794, Fulton began to do some research of his own. He wrote a letter to Matthew Boulton and James Watt, the pioneers of steam-engine development, and asked about the cost of purchasing a three- or four-horsepower steam engine. He also asked how long it would take to build such an engine, what size boat would be required to hold it, and how much coal the engine would consume.

A Mechanical Excavator

When Boulton and Watt never replied to Fulton's letter, and he did not write to them again. Instead, he devoted his attention to a new project. In 1794, he had designed a machine that could be used to dig canals, and he began to focus on perfecting

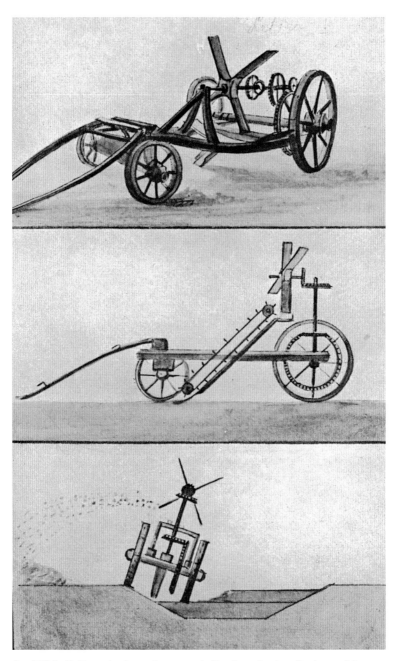

In 1794, Fulton designed a canal-digging device that would accomplish much more than the existing system of men who dug with shovels.

Fulton's book about canals was published in 1796. The work included a wealth of information on canal construction and navigation as well as Fulton's own drawings.

his design. The canal-digging device that Fulton envisioned would be powered by four horses, which pulled a frame with four wheels. Attached to the frame would be a curved container that scooped the dirt as the horses moved. Fulton believed that his device would work much faster than the current method, which involved men using shovels. He also claimed that his invention would result in much lower labor costs. His work never progressed beyond paper, however, and he never bothered to apply for a patent. His reasons for this are unknown, but according to biographer H.W. Dickinson, the invention was both crude and impractical. Thus, Dickinson says, it was likely that Fulton did not try to patent it because after analyzing his design he realized the machine was destined to fail.

Fulton as Author

Even though Fulton abandoned his plans for a canal-digging machine, his intense interest in canals continued. In fact, he was inspired to write a book about them. In 1796 he published *A Treatise on the Improvement of Canal Navigation*, which included nearly160 pages of text and his own drawings. The book listed "Robert Fulton, Civil Engineer" as the author, and it covered such topics as the advantages of canal transportation, canal construction and navigation, and the advantages of small canals. It also included detailed information about inclined planes, as well as Fulton's drawings of a variety of iron bridges and designs for transportation channels known as aqueducts. The book did not, however, include any reference to Fulton's canal-digging machine.

One of the most unusual features of Treatise was its preface, because Fulton used it to explain his thoughts about inventions, and who actually "owned" them. He stated his belief that inventions were rarely the result of one person's idea, but instead were the product of accumulated knowledge and experience. In Cynthia Owen Philip's biography, she explains Fulton's perspective: "An invention was for him the product of a long process of knowledge gathering. . . . The wide community of scientists and mechanics provided the basic materials; the creative role of the individual was to improve on them by discovering new and useful relationships among them."[9] Fulton's belief was not shared by most scientists and inventors, who were convinced that inventions were only credible if they were unique, original ideas. Thus, Fulton's ideas were unpopular with many of these people.

Decision to Leave England

In spite of Fulton's controversial viewpoints on inventions, his book was generally well received. Even the Earl of Stanhope was excited about it, and wrote the following in a letter to him: "Your book about Canals, has set me, you see, on fire. . . . So I hope that at last, I shall burn to some purpose, provided you keep on blowing the Fire, as you have done."[10] Yet even though reactions to the book were favorable, it did not bring Fulton the success or fame he had hoped for. His financial situation was growing bleak, as he had very little money left. In late 1796 he returned to London. When he was unsuccessful at finding work there, he wrote to Stanhope and pleaded for a loan. There are no records to show whether Stanhope ever answered him.

"Your book about Canals, has set me, you see, on fire..."

—THE EARL OF STANHOPE, IN A 1796 LETTER TO FULTON

Fulton thought about returning to America. Not only was he homesick for the country where he was born, he knew that America was considered a land of opportunity. It was still young and was growing fast. That meant there was great potential for canal transportation, and because of that, he would have a better chance of putting his knowledge about canals into practice. He made plans to sail for home.

For unknown reasons, Fulton changed his travel plans at the last minute. Instead of returning to America, he decided to cross the English Channel and spend some time in France. He did not know how long he would stay, but he believed it would be for less than a year.

Paris

Fulton arrived in France in June 1797. When he arrived in Paris, he found lodging in a boarding house. During his stay, Fulton became acquainted with Ruth Barlow, and later he met her husband, Joel. The three soon became very close friends. When the Barlows moved to a house on Paris's Left Bank, they invited Fulton to move in with them and he gladly accepted their offer.

Joel and Ruth Barlow were worldly, sophisticated people who were older than Fulton, and who had

Joel Barlow believed that a boiler he developed could be used with a steamboat engine. When Fulton lived in Paris, he and Barlow became close friends.

no children. They valued his friendship and enjoyed his company immensely, and he felt the same about them. From the Barlows he learned a great deal about mathematics, physics, chemistry, and other sciences. They also taught him how to speak fluent French, as well as some Italian and German. They introduced him to their circle of influential friends, including people who were well known in the areas of science, literature, and politics.

Like Fulton, Joel Barlow was an ambitious man who was interested in mechanical gadgets and inventions. He and Fulton shared much in common and enjoyed many interesting conversations. Several years before, Barlow had developed a

25

boiler and was granted a French patent for it. He believed that the boiler would be suitable for use with a steamboat engine, and he was very enthusiastic about the potential of steam engines as a way to power boats.

Another of Fulton's close friends was an English poet and inventor named Edmund Cartwright. He and Fulton had become acquainted in London, and during Fulton's stay in France, the two men regularly corresponded with each other. Fulton told Cartwright about life in France, and he described the city of Paris in great detail. His letters also discussed the current war between France and England. For centuries, the two countries had considered each other enemies and they had engaged in numerous wars. One such war had broken out in 1793, and it continued to rage on. Fulton wrote of his observations that despite the battles in other parts of the country, in Paris it seemed as though no one was even aware of the war at all. Instead, he described a city where everything was "gay and joyous."

"A Curious Machine for Mending . . . Politics"

Fulton had long been against war, and on more than one occasion he had spoken out publicly against it. As loyal supporter of free trade between countries, he was especially vocal about Europe's

Edmund Cartwright, an English inventor and poet, shared his observations on the war between England and France in his correspondence with Fulton.

naval warships. In an effort to control ocean traffic, these warships frequently attacked merchant ships. For that reason, Fulton believed they were the biggest hindrance to free trade. In the fall of 1797, Fulton wrote an essay entitled "Thoughts on Free Trade," in which he bluntly declared that all trade barriers should be removed. In several later publications, Fulton used even stronger words to protest the war, and he continued to voice his opposition to any sort of trade barriers.

Considering Fulton's antiwar position, the focus of his attention in late 1797 was quite unusual: He intended to develop a submarine that was armed with explosive minelike devices that he called "torpedoes." He believed that not only would armed submarines give France the means to destroy enemy warships, they were also the answer to ending all war. In a letter to Cartwright, he referred to the submarine as "a curious machine for mending the system of politics and applying manual labor to advantage."[11] Fulton believed that France, by putting sub-

> "If this man is supported, he will give us the liberty of the seas and a system of interior public improvements superior to what has been seen in any country."
>
> —JOEL BARLOW, IN AN 1807 LETTER TO PRESIDENT THOMAS JEFFERSON ABOUT FULTON'S TORPEDOES

marines into operation, could destroy the British navy and thus restore free trade. Whether he considered that submarines could also be used to destroy merchant ships—which would, in turn, damage free trade—is not known. Rather, Fulton's mind seemed to be on only one thing, and that was how France could benefit from a destructive underwater ship. He believed that developing such a ship would bring him both fame and wealth.

The First Submarine

When Fulton envisioned his submarine in late 1797, he was not the first person to do so. For centuries people had been fascinated with the idea of underwater ships that could carry

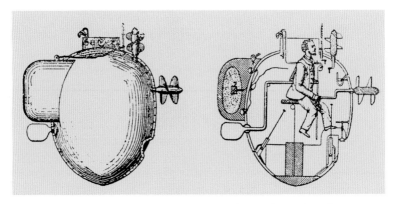

In 1776, David Bushnell imagined the first submarine, the American Turtle. *The American inventor's design (pictured) shows was a one-man vessel equipped with a torpedo.*

weapons. None, however, had ever progressed beyond the idea phase. Then in 1776, the year the United States declared its independence from England, an American named David Bushnell made the idea a reality. He designed and built a submarine called the *American Turtle*. It was a small vessel, designed for just one man, and was armed with a time-activated bomb that Bushnell called a torpedo. After several unsuccessful experiments, however, the *Turtle* sank and Bushnell never repaired it. He also gave up on his idea of developing torpedo-armed submarines.

The Nautilus

Whether Fulton copied Bushnell's idea or came up with the idea himself is not known, although Fulton claimed that the invention was exclusively his. Since information about Bushnell's submarine was not released to the public until 1799, it is doubtful that Fulton was aware of it.

Fulton designed a submarine that could hold a crew of three men and was twenty feet long, which was nearly three times the size of Bushnell's *Turtle*. When the submarine was underwater, it would be moved by hand-cranked propellers. Fulton believed it would be able to stay under the water for about three hours, and light would be provided by candles.

On the surface of the water, the submarine would be propelled either by hand cranks or sails.

In December 1797, Fulton prepared a proposal about the submarine, which he called the *Nautulus* (he later changed the spelling to "Nautilus"), and sent the document to the French government. In a separate letter, he boasted about the *Nautilus*'s potential to destroy the entire British navy and restore freedom to the seas. Fulton did not provide details about the vessel's construction, nor did he explain exactly how it would accomplish such an extraordinary feat. He did, however, offer to explain the mechanics of the *Nautilus* to someone—such as the celebrated French general, Napoleon Bonaparte—who would be capable of understanding technical things. Fulton's expectation was that the French government would be so intrigued with his submarine idea that they would be unable to resist it. In turn, he believed that he would become a very rich man.

At first, some French officials were interested in Fulton's idea of an underwater warship. In February 1798, however, he

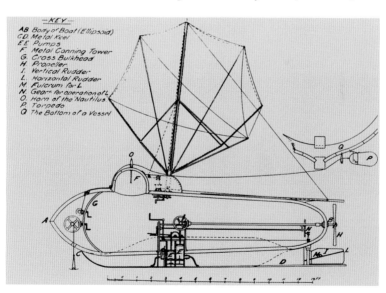

--KEY--
AB Body of Boat (Ellipsoid)
CD Metal Keel
EE Pumps
F. Metal Conning Tower
G. Cross Bulkhead
H. Propeller
I. Vertical Rudder
L. Horizontal Rudder
M. Fulcrum for L
N. Gears for operation of L
O. Horn of the 'Nautilus'
P. Torpedo
Q The Bottom of a Vessel

Fulton designed the Nautilus *in 1797. His submarine was twenty feet long, held three men, and was powered by hand-cranked propellers while underwater.*

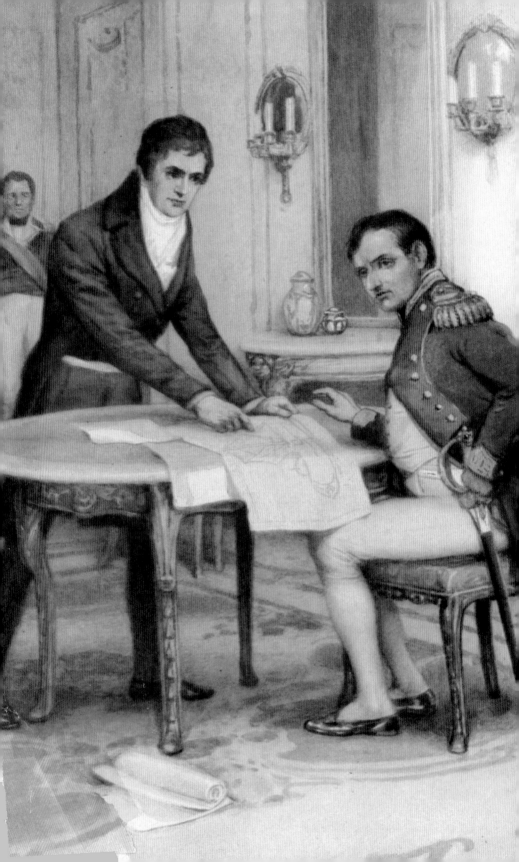

received a disappointing letter from France's Marine Ministry. The letter said that French government officials were not interested in his proposal.

A Miniature Submarine

Fulton refused to give up. In July 1798, he wrote directly to Bonaparte, and he also submitted another proposal to the French government. Along with the proposal, he enclosed the submarine plans he had drawn. As he had done before, he boldly claimed that his creation would allow France to destroy the English navy and then go on to become the European leader. He also stated that he had built a "beautiful model of the *Nautilus* five feet long complete in all its parts,"[12] and he invited French officials to attend a demonstration and see it for themselves. This time, he captured their attention.

In August, Fulton demonstrated his miniature submarine for a commission of French officials. He began by explaining the principles behind the *Nautilus*, and then he operated the craft in a huge basin of water. His audience was extremely pleased with what they observed. A month later, they wrote a review of the demonstration, in which they praised Fulton. They compared the *Nautilus* with a fish that swam underwater with only its tail above the surface, and they said the submarine had qualities that resembled a fish as much as a boat. In fact, they called it a *bateau-poisson*, the French words for " boat-fish." The report also offered some suggestions for improvements to the underwater craft, and it concluded with a recommendation to the French government: "The Commission invites the Minister of Marine and of the Colonies to authorise citizen Fulton to make the machine, the model of which he has produced, and grant him the necessary [financing]. It cannot be doubted that, with the same brains that have been put into its conception, the elegance and solidity of the different mechanisms . . . [Fulton] would be able to construct the full-sized machine in a manner equally ingenious."[13]

Opposite: *Fulton presented his submarine design to Napoléon Bonaparte and the French government as a machine that would defeat England in the war.*

From Hope to Despair

Fulton, however, did not became aware of the commission's favorable report right away. In fact, it was several months before he heard from them, and he became frustrated. He wrote a series of letters to the commission, but he received no response. Finally, in October 1798, he sent them an angry letter. He reminded them of their commitment to his project and demanded an answer. When he did not hear back, he sent a formal plan, in which he proposed to build a full-sized submarine at his own expense. He explained that his intent was to launch the vessel in the sea. As soon as it destroyed or captured one enemy warship, Fulton would be paid five hundred thousand francs, the equivalent of over one hundred thousand dollars in American money. When he still received no reply, he sent a series of letters to

Fulton became frustrated when the French did not respond to his proposals and felt he had reached a roadblock in his development of the submarine.

French officials—and again, he heard nothing in return. Fulton felt as though he had been badly deceived.

The commission did nothing with Fulton's letters and proposals except forward them to the Marine Ministry, which did not take any action. No one provided Fulton with an explanation of why his submarine was delayed, or worse, why it had become a dead issue. He did not plan to give up, but he could no longer count on receiving income from the *Nautilus* as he had expected. Instead, he found it necessary to focus his energy and creativity in other directions.

The First Panorama in Paris

Desperate for a way to earn money, Fulton began to consider various ideas. He remembered the panoramas he had seen while living in London, and how he had long been fascinated with them. Panoramas were huge landscape paintings that were displayed on buildings and in public settings. The first one ever created and publicly displayed was painted by an artist named Robert Barker, and he had received an English patent for it in 1787. Later, Barker created several more panoramas in London, one of which was ninety feet in diameter. To Fulton, the creations were works of artistic genius.

There were no panoramas in Paris, and Fulton wanted to develop one. He envisioned a "circular picture without boundaries and the method of painting all the countryside, all the towns and villages . . . and other objects which can be seen from the summit of a mountain or a tower."[14] Because Parisians placed such a high value on art and were always interested in

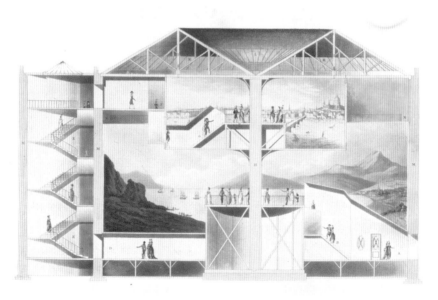

Fulton acquired a panorama patent so he could introduce the giant paintings to Paris. He profited financially when his panorama became one of the city's most popular attractions.

34

anything new and exciting, Fulton believed his panorama would be immensely popular. He also believed that it would be a moneymaker for him. He applied for a French patent, and it was granted in April 1799.

The first step was to build a structure where the panorama would be displayed. In the center of Paris, Fulton supervised the construction of a circular building forty-six feet in diameter. Huge pieces of canvas covered the interior walls of the building. The scene that was painted on the canvas was of a devastating fire in Moscow, Russia, one of many that occurred in the seventeenth and eighteenth centuries. The painting was referred to as *l'Incendie de Moscow*, or "Burning of Moscow."

Even though Fulton was a talented and accomplished artist, he did not paint the panorama himself. Instead, he believed it would be completed faster—and would thus bring him profits more quickly—if he hired a team of four artists to do the work, so that is what he did.

> "The mechanic should sit down among levers, screws, wedges, wheels etc. like a poet among the letters of the alphabet, considering them as the exhibition of his thoughts; in which a new arrangement transmits a new idea to the world."
>
> —ROBERT FULTON

As Fulton had hoped, when his panorama was complete it was an immediate success. In fact, it became one of the most popular attractions in Paris and was described favorably in a tourist guidebook: "Patrons enter through a dark tunnel and when they reach the painting, lighted by a central clerestory window, become so absorbed in the . . . view that they forget it is a mere illusion. . . . A stranger greets it with a sigh and takes leave of it regretfully."[15] Less than a year after Fulton had received his patent, he sold it to an American, but he continued to receive a portion of the income. As he had hoped, the panorama had become profitable for him.

A Machine for Making Rope

While Fulton completed work on his panorama, he also developed another creation: a machine for making rope. At that time rope was made entirely by hand by men who were called "ropewalkers." The men traveled along an area known as a "ropewalk," facing backwards and walking away from spinning wheels. As they walked, they twisted and stretched handfuls of hemp (a natural fiber) into a long coil, thereby forming the rope. The process was both difficult and time-consuming, and the job was so strenuous that men could work only in short shifts. Fulton knew that ships needed a constant supply of rope, so there was a great demand for it. He believed it made sense to make rope mechanically instead of manually. Because both money and time would be saved, Fulton thought a rope-making machine would be a very profitable invention.

Several years before, Fulton's friend Edmund Cartwright had created and patented his own rope-making machine that he called a "cordelier." In June 1798, while Fulton waited to find out the fate of his *Nautilus*, he had written to Cartwright and

Fulton designed a rope-making machine to replace ropewalkers (pictured), men who walked away from spinning wheels to twist and form rope.

In 1799 Fulton once again turned his energies to the Nautilus *and urged the French government to reconsider his requests.*

described the machine that he wanted to create. It would be similar to Cartwright's cordelier, but Fulton would design his own version. Once it was built, he would apply for a French patent. At that time, granting patents for products invented in other countries was an acceptable and encouraged practice in France. The French government saw it as a way to stimulate and build the country's economy.

Fulton built a model of the rope-making machine and he was granted a French patent in May 1799. Because of problems with financing, however, and a failed partnership with an acquaintance, Fulton's creation never achieved much success. It also did not bring him the financial reward for which he had hoped.

Renewed Focus on Submarines

Even as Fulton worked diligently on his inventions, he never gave up hope on the *Nautilus*. He had not forgotten the promises that the French government had made to him. In July 1799, Fulton sent a letter in which he urged French officials to take advantage of his designs. He again registered that he was willing to build the *Nautilus* at his own expense, and that his only motivation was "the happiness of having contributed to the re-establishment of peace, the freedom of the seas and of commerce."[16] The group who reviewed Fulton's offer felt positively about it and recommended that he be given permission to build and operate the submarine. As before, however, nothing happened, and Fulton was furious.

The cover of this French magazine depicts the interior of Fulton's Nautilus, *which embarked on its maiden voyage in the River Seine in 1801.*

Finally he had had enough. He wrote another angry letter to French officials, and along with it he enclosed an essay he had written, entitled "Observations on the Moral Effects of the *Nautilus* Should It Be Employed with Success." Once more, he presented his case for the submarine and the benefits it would bring to France. For the first time, though, his writing took on a threatening tone. He stated that he hoped, for the sake of France, that it would not become necessary for him to look to America or other countries for support of the *Nautilus*. In other words, if France was not interested, he would take his idea elsewhere.

Test on the Seine

Fulton's threatening letter, instead, actually succeeded in getting the French officials' verbal support for his project. He was not given the promise of future financial backing, but still he was filled with a new sense of purpose. He believed that there was no way the government could possibly refuse to endorse his submarine. So, he hired Jacques Périer, one of France's most respected machine manufacturers, to turn his designs into a real underwater boat.

Throughout the winter of 1800, Périer built the *Nautilus*, and Fulton supervised his work. By spring the submarine was complete, and Fulton scheduled a demonstration for June 13. It was to be held on the River Seine in Paris, and Fulton sent personal invitations to government officials and other prominent citizens. He also hoped that word would spread so that many curious spectators would attend the event.

Fulton was not disappointed. A large crowd of people gathered on the banks of the Seine, anxiously awaiting his demonstration of the *Nautilus*. They watched the boat plunge under the water, stay down for a while, and then bob back up to the surface. Then it plunged again, resurfaced, and sailed across the water for shore. The experiment had been a success, and Fulton was ecstatic. The next test, however, would be the biggest challenge—proving that the submarine could destroy an enemy ship.

Taking on the British

After his successful demonstration, Fulton took the *Nautilus* to Rouen, a city north of Paris that was also located on the Seine. He spent some time testing the boat, and then he moved to Le Havre, a town that had better access to the English Channel. Fulton conducted additional tests there and continued perfecting the vessel's features, including the torpedo system. Finally, his submarine was ready to be tested in the open sea against an English warship. Fulton did not seem concerned about the odds against him—that he was just one man in one small boat, facing the world's most powerful navy. He was confident that his submarine could conquer any warships, and he was ready for the challenge ahead.

Fulton set out in search of English ships (pictured) in order to test his battle-ready submarine.

On September 12, 1800, Fulton set out for La Hogue, where he expected to find English ships. He arrived five days later at a small harbor named Growan, where he remained for more than a month. Because of severe wind and waves, he was forced to spend most of his time close to the shoreline, rather than venturing out too far into the sea. He spotted two English ships that were anchored nearby, and twice he tried to approach them with the intent of blowing them up. Both times, however, the ships left before he could reach them. He later wrote that he was not sure whether it was a coincidence that the ships sailed away, or if they had deliberately tried to escape from him.

With winter only a short time away, Fulton decided to leave the *Nautilus* in Growan and return to Paris. He was concerned that the *Nautilus's* construction would not be able to withstand winter's bad weather and rough seas. He had not been able to get close enough to a ship to destroy one, but he did not feel defeated. He had no intention of giving up on the project that had been his focus for more than three years.

The End of the Line

Although his boat had not yet destroyed even one warship, Fulton felt that his experiments had been a success. He later wrote his thoughts about this: "I look upon the most difficult part of the work as done. Navigation under water is an operation whose possibility is proven, and it can be said that a new series of ideas have just been born as to the means for preventing naval wars or rather of hindering them in the future."[17] In the spring of 1801, Fulton went back to Growan, where he discovered that the *Nautilus* had suffered heavy damage during the winter. He spent the spring and summer months making repairs and testing it. Then, for reasons that are unknown, he disassembled the boat, sold some of the parts, and destroyed the rest.

Fulton wrote to French officials and provided them with a master plan, which contained explicit details of how he intended to destroy the English naval fleet. He talked at great length about the possibilities for underwater warfare. He also spoke of his desire to have larger submarines built and how powerful those ships would be. What he did not mention, however, was that he had already destroyed the *Nautilus*—a vessel in which the French government had invested money.

When Bonaparte himself asked to see the submarine, Fulton could no longer hide what he had done. He wrote back and explained: "When I finished my experiments, She leaked very much, and being but an imperfect engine, I did not think her further useful, hence I took her to pieces."[18] Fulton confessed that after he took the boat apart he had sold the iron, lead, and cylinders. The boat was dissembled, and nothing remained of it. Thus, Fulton lost credibility with French officials, and he was notified that France was no longer interested in his ideas about underwater warfare.

An Important Meeting

Fulton's submarine plans had failed, and he was downhearted. He had hoped for fame and fortune and he had not even come close to achieving his goals. He and the Barlows considered moving back to America, where Fulton thought perhaps he could resume his work with canals. Then, a chance meeting with a distinguished American during the early part of 1802 gave Fulton a renewed sense of purpose.

The man's name was Robert Livingston, and he was powerful influential, and extremely wealthy. A resident of New York, Livingston was the U.S. minister to France and had recently arrived in Paris with his family. Livingston knew about Fulton, and was impressed with the work he had done with submarines and torpedoes. As soon as Fulton became aware of Livingston's goal—building a steamboat—he was captivated with the idea.

Early Steamboat Experiments

Livingston had already made several attempts to build a steamboat, but they had failed. Others before him had tried and failed as well. The first to come close was a Frenchman named Claude-François–Dorothée Jouffroy d'Abbans, who built a steamboat in the early 1780s. In 1783, he launched his boat on the River Saône in France. It chugged along the river at a very slow pace for fifteen minutes. Then, apparently because the engine was too heavy for the boat, the hull suddenly split apart and the vessel barely made it to shore. Jouffroy planned to build another boat, but he could not get the financial backing.

Another man who had built a steamboat was an American named John Fitch. In 1790, after trial runs proved successful, Fitch advertised that his boat was ready to carry passengers along the Delaware River. He made regular trips for an entire summer, traveling between Philadelphia and Trenton, New Jersey. His boat moved so slowly, however, that no one wanted to ride on it. Passengers preferred to travel either by sailboat or by stagecoach. Fitch eventually ran out of money and abandoned his idea of operating a steamboat line. He never built another boat.

Robert Livingston, the U.S. minister to France, had tried unsuccessfully to build a functional steamboat before he entered into a partnership with Fulton in 1802.

The Partnership

In the following years, other men toyed with building steamboats, but they were no more successful than Jouffroy or Fitch had been. Unlike those before him, however, Livingston refused to be discouraged by past failures. His interest in building a steamboat was more intense than ever—especially after he met Fulton. The two men soon found that they shared many things in common. They both had a keen interest in mechanical things, and they were both interested in the potential of steamboat transportation.

On October 10, 1802, Livingston and Fulton signed a partnership agreement, in which they spelled out the plans for the steamboat and their financial arrangement. Fulton would design a vessel that was one hundred twenty feet long, traveled

To help develop his steamboat, Fulton asked borrow a steam engine (pictured) designed by Watt and Boulton. The two men, however, denied his request.

at a speed of eight miles per hour, and had the capacity to carry sixty passengers. He would go to England, where the best steam engines were made, and attempt to borrow a steam engine from Boulton and Watt. He would then supervise the construction of a prototype (full-sized model) of the steamboat. If the tests with the prototype were successful, Fulton would travel to the United States and oversee the construction of a real boat that would travel the Hudson River in New York.

From Disaster to Triumph

Fulton's spirits were dampened when Boulton and Watt refused his request to borrow a steam engine, but he did not let that stop him. Instead, he hired two French craftsmen to build an engine. Together, Fulton and the craftsmen worked throughout the winter and spring of 1803 to construct the steamboat.

In May, the boat was finished. Fulton moored it in the Seine, in full view of the people of Paris, who were curious about the strange-looking vessel. In her biography of Fulton, Cynthia Owen Philip describes the boat: "It looked like a floating furnace with two great Catherine wheels attached to the sides, a vehicle more appropriate for a fireworks display than for carrying flesh-and-blood passengers and valuable cargo."[19] Fulton was eager to launch his steamboat and show it off. Before he was able to do that, however, disaster struck one night while he slept. He was awakened by a messenger who told him that the boat had been badly smashed and had sunk to the bottom of the river. No one knew for sure what had happened, but the damage was so bad that it appeared to be the work of vandals. Fulton, feeling more despondent than he

> "If this man is supported, he will give us the liberty of the seas and a system of interior public improvements superior to what has been seen in any country."
>
> —JOEL BARLOW, IN AN 1807 LETTER TO PRESIDENT THOMAS JEFFERSON ABOUT FULTON'S TORPEDOES

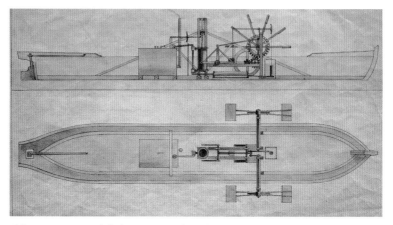

After a successful demonstration in 1803, Paris newspapers hailed Fulton's steamboat (design above) as a "complete and brilliant success."

ever had, worked for twenty-four hours to salvage what was left of his vessel. He found that the engine had not been damaged, but the boat needed to be completely rebuilt.

After nearly three months of work, Fulton was once again ready for a demonstration. On August 9, 1803, he fired up the steam engine and piloted the vessel up and down the Seine, in front of many curious spectators. A select group of government officials and prominent citizens rode as passengers in two boats that Fulton towed behind the steamboat. The trial run went perfectly and was later declared by a Paris newspaper to be a "complete and brilliant success." The newspaper also referred to Fulton as a "celebrated mechanic," and it declared that the steamboat would have "important consequences for the commerce and internal navigation of France."[20]

Remarkable Turn of Events

Fulton was encouraged by his successful test run. He decided his next step would be to travel to the United States, as he and Livingston had agreed, where he would build another steamboat. He wrote a letter to Boulton and Watt, in which he inquired about having a steam engine built and then shipped to New York. They replied to his letter and expressed their regrets at not being able to get an export permit from the British government. Fulton wrote several letters of protest to the British government. He did not pursue the matter any further, though, because something unrelated to steamboats had captured his attention: a visit by an agent from the British secret service.

The agent called himself "Mr. Smith," and he had come to Paris to present Fulton with an offer. British officials were well aware of Fulton's knowledge and expertise in submarine development. They were familiar with his work on the *Nautilus*, and they also knew that the French government had turned down his ideas. So, they proposed that he build submarines for the British government.

The two men continued their negotiations in secret meetings. Then in March 1804, they arrived at a deal, and Fulton agreed to go to England. The way he viewed it, the French government had its chance and was obviously not interested in his designs. He was free to build submarines for whomever he wanted. He would, therefore, build them for the British navy. In late April, he left Paris and arrived in London about two weeks later.

Back in England

As soon as Fulton was back in England, he drew up plans for a submarine and torpedoes and submitted them to the British government. To his dismay, the submarine plans were rejected within a month. British officials did not believe it was necessary to pay for an expensive and time-consuming submarine project when, as they saw it, the torpedoes could be carried by ordinary boats. They were interested only in Fulton's plans for the torpedoes. Fulton was angry and disappointed. He had counted on being paid for the submarine, and this meant he would receive much less money than he had planned. Still, he would make some money from the sale of his torpedoes, so he decided to go ahead and build them.

Fulton had his first underwater weapons built by the fall of 1804, and they were ready to test on enemy warships. Between October 1804 and October 1805, he supervised multiple tests of the torpedoes. Most of the tests failed when very little damage was done to the targets. Finally, during the last test, Fulton

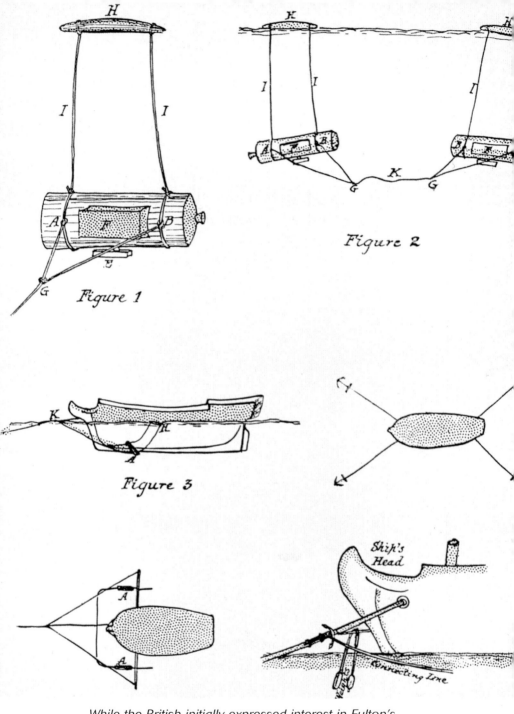

Figure 1

Figure 2

Figure 3

Ship's Head

Connecting Line

While the British initially expressed interest in Fulton's torpedoes, they eventually decided the weapons were too expensive.

was finally able to show the destructive powers of his torpedoes. By then, however, the British government had lost interest. The officials were not convinced that the weapons would be as effective as they had hoped and, as with the submarine, they believed the benefits did not justify the expense. They refused to pay for any further development. Fulton wrote threatening letters to them, which the officials ignored. Finally, in the fall of 1806, they agreed to a financial settlement to cover Fulton's time and expenses. Fulton, not nearly as rich as he had hoped but still financially secure, made plans to return to America. He booked passage on a ship called the *Windsor Castle*, and in late October 1806, he started on the long journey home.

Full Steam Ahead

Fulton's ship arrived in New York City on December 13, 1806. After being in Europe for so many years, he was astounded at the changes that had taken place while he was gone. The city now had a population of over eighty thousand people, and he could see buildings and homes under construction everywhere he looked. Even the river was crowded, with more boats than he had ever seen before. It seemed as though there was a buzz of activity in every corner of the city. Fulton was glad to be back.

When he arrived in New York, one of the first things he did was write a letter to Robert Livingston, saying that he was ready to go ahead with the steamboat project. During his time in England, Fulton had designed the exact steam engine he wanted, and then hired Matthew Boulton (Watt had since retired) to build it for him. The British government had granted Fulton permission to export the engine, and he had it shipped to America. It now awaited him in a New York warehouse.

By mid-March of 1807, work on the new steamboat had begun. Fulton retrieved the engine from storage, and he hired a well-known shipbuilder to build the boat. He told Livingston that he expected the project to take about four months to complete.

By the end of July, Fulton's steamboat was ready for its first test. On August 9, 1807, he took the boat out and ran it one mile up the East River and back. He was happy with how well it performed, and all he needed to do was make adjustments to

the paddlewheels, water pump, and engine. A week later, Fulton took the steamboat out for a final test. Once again, it ran exactly as he had planned, and he was totally confident in its ability to make the long trip upriver to Albany and back. The next day, August 17, 1807, Fulton made his historic maiden voyage on the steamboat he later named the *North River*.

In 1807, Fulton and forty passengers embarked on his steamboat's famous journey from New York City to Albany and back along the Hudson River.

Romantic Notions

About forty guests rode along on the famous Hudson River steamboat journey. One of them was a young woman named Harriet Livingston, who was a cousin of Fulton's partner, Robert Livingston. Harriet was elegant and intelligent, known for her artistic talent as well as her skills at playing the harp. It

During the steamboat's maiden voyage, Fulton fell in love with Harriet Livingston.

is not known whether she and Fulton had ever met before, but he became so fond of her during the trip that he decided he wanted to marry her.

Alice Crary Sutcliffe, Fulton's great-granddaughter, writes of a conversation Fulton was said to have had with Robert Livingston, in which he asked: "Is it presumptuous in me to aspire to the hand of Miss Harriet Livingston?" Livingston replied by saying, "By no means, her father may object because you are a humble and poor inventor, and the family may object—but if Harriet does not object,—and she seems to have a world of good sense,—go ahead, and my best wishes and blessings go with you."[21] Fulton did propose to Harriet, and to his delight, she agreed to marry him.

Commercial Steamboat Operation

Fulton and his future wife did not see much of each other in the months following the *North River* trip. She stayed at Clermont, the Livingston family mansion, while he busied himself with making repairs to the steamboat to prepare it for passenger travel. On September 2, 1807, he placed advertisements in two New York newspapers: the *Albany Gazette* and the *Evening Post*. He announced that the steamboat would make regular trips to Albany and back, and that the service would begin on September 4.

Fulton's new business venture was an immediate success. He carried twelve passengers on his first trip, and by October, as many as ninety people traveled with him. His steamboat continued to operate until November 19, when the Hudson River froze over. In less than three months, Fulton's commercial steamboat operation had become profitable, and he was confident that it would make even more money in the future.

The winter of 1808 was a busy and eventful season for Fulton. On January 7, he and Harriet Livingston were married. Their wedding took place in the parlor at Teviotdale, one of the Livingston family homes. Afterward, the couple moved into the Teviotdale mansion, and Fulton spent much of the winter repairing and refurbishing the *North River*. He decided that it would be even more attractive to passengers if it had luxurious accommodations. He added such features as polished oak railings, comfortable sofas, mahogany tables, and enough sleeping berths for nearly eighty people. By spring, he was ready for another busy boating season.

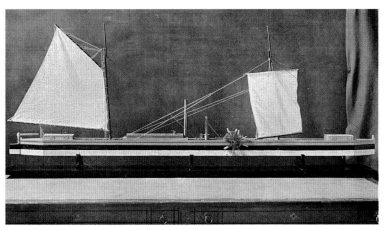

In September 1807, Fulton started a steamboat business. His steamboat carried as many as ninety people on each trip between New York City and Albany.

Expanding the Fleet

Throughout the following years, Fulton designed and built more steamboats. One of these was the *Paragon*, a large boat that was one hundred seventy feet long and twenty-eight feet wide. The *Paragon* was an elegant vessel with two mahogany staircases, carpeting, and curtains made of fringed muslin and silk. There were enough beds to accommodate more than one hundred passengers, plus crew members and servants, and the sleeping cabins were spacious, with large windows and sky-lights. All meals were served on china dishes. Fulton believed that no boat could compare to his *Paragon*, which he called a "floating palace."

Other steamboats that Fulton added to his fleet included *Car of Neptune*, the *Raritan*, the *Firefly*, and the *Jersey*. In September 1811, he completed the *New Orleans*, a steamboat that expanded his operations outside of New York and into the Mississippi River.

As Fulton's fleet of steamboats continued to grow, his family grew as well. His son, Robert Barlow, named after Joel Barlow, was born in October 1808, and his daughter. Julia was born in

This print depicts the Fulton's "floating palace," the Paragon. *The luxurious steamboat could hold more than one hundred people.*

April 1811. Then in August 1812, another daughter was born, and the Fultons named her Cornelia, after Harriet's mother. In a letter to Robert Livingston, Fulton referred to his family as "happy as doves in a basket."[22]

Continued Fascination with Weaponry

As content as Fulton seemed to be with his family and his successful steamboat operation, one area of his life was still unfulfilled: his desire to design and sell underwater weapons. He had not succeeded with either the French or British governments, but that did not mean that he had given up. In the six years since he had returned to America, he had been working on torpedo designs at the same time that he designed and built steamboats. Even though America and England were no longer at war with each other, American ships were still in danger of attack while at sea. Also, American ports needed to be protected. Fulton believed that his torpedoes were the answer.

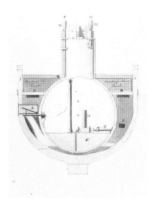

Fulton drew this image of a submarine and remained fascinated by underwater warfare. The U.S. Navy, however, was not interested in Fulton's designs.

On several occasions, he demonstrated the power of his underwater weapons for officials from the government and the navy, but no one was especially impressed. In 1810, he published a booklet entitled *Torpedo War and Submarine Explosions*, in which he strongly stated that torpedoes were the country's best chance for protection. He provided details about the weapons he had designed and built, as well as those he proposed for the future. Naval officials remained uninterested. Fulton was offended by their treatment of him, which he described as cold. One naval officer referred to Fulton's ideas about torpedo warfare as "the most impractical scheme to have originated in the brain of a man not actually out of his mind."[23]

Contrary to what the navy thought, members of Congress believed that Fulton's ideas might work, and they provided him with money to develop some experimental torpedoes. At a public demonstration, however, the weapons failed to perform as Fulton had promised. He was later notified that the government would not rely on his underwater weapon system for protection of its ships.

Fulton was disappointed, but he was still convinced that he would someday have a chance to prove the worth of his weapons. In 1812, when America declared war on Great Britain and the War of 1812 began, he believed he would finally get that chance. He began to write to war officials about his ideas, but he was not successful in convincing them. Vowing not to give up, he put his plans on hold temporarily and turned his attention back to his steamboat business.

Bittersweet Year

By 1813, Fulton had a fleet of steamboats in full operation and more in development. He had also designed and built a dry dock in Jersey City, New Jersey, which was the first facility of its kind in the country. Fulton's dry dock was a three-building complex where boats and engines could be built. It contained a model shop, a blacksmith's shop, a boiler shop, and a variety of specialized boat- and engine-building tools and machinery. His steamboat operation was thriving and he was pleased with his success. He was also pleased with the wealth it had brought him.

Not all aspects of Fulton's life were happy, however. The year 1813 also brought him great sadness because he lost two of his closest friends. In February, Robert Livingston suffered a stroke and died. On the very same day that Fulton received the news about Livingston, he was also informed that Joel Barlow had died while visiting Poland. Fulton was devastated, and he described his grief in a letter to Harriet's brother: "This melancholy news arrived to me on the same day, to me it is an immense loss. . . . Few men have lost 2 such companions and sincere friends in the short space of 2 months. . . . I am much oppressed with sorrow." [24]

Fulton used his knowledge of steam engines (pictured) to build a steam frigate, or warship, for the U.S. Congress.

In spite of his depression over the loss of his friends, Fulton managed to keep going. In July, he became a father for the fourth time when Harriet delivered a baby girl named Mary. In addition to caring for his family, he also needed to focus on his business. He had continued to add to his fleet of steamboats with the addition of the *Hope*, the *Richmond*, and the *Washington*. He also built another elegant boat called the *Fulton*, and three new steam ferries called the *York*, the *Jersey*, and the *Nassau*. These ferries were large enough to carry not only people, but also horses and carriages. By May 1814, the *Nassau* alone was making as many as forty trips per day, carrying over five hundred passengers. His steamboat operation was thriving.

A Steam-Powered Warship

There was also another steamboat on Fulton's mind-one that combined his experience with steam transportation and his interest in powerful weapons. The previous December, he had designed a steam frigate, or warship. He envisioned a vessel that weighed nearly two hundred fifty tons, which was shielded with thick wooden planks to protect it against attacks by enemy ships. It would also feature a gun deck that held as many as thirty cannons. In March 1814, Fulton was granted a patent for the steam frigate, and a short time later he asked

Congress to pay for him to build it. Much to his delight, they agreed. He immediately began to build the ship, and worked night and day as he personally supervised every detail of its construction.

Four months later, Fulton's steam frigate was complete except for its engine. On October 29, 1814, the vessel was launched into the East River in a public demonstration. A huge crowd of curious spectators attended, and Cynthia Owen Philip

describes the excitement in the air: "The river and bay were filled with anchored vessels of war, festooned with all their colors. Man-powered craft and sailboats threaded their way among them. To those lucky enough to have procured places in advance, the horse-propelled ferry lying off Delancey Street afforded a fine view. Bands played aboard Fulton's steamboats as they 'skimmed along as if by enchantment.' The air vibrated with the excitement of the glorious event. At high tide, amid the roar of cannon and the shouts of 20,000 people, the great hull plunged into the water."[25]

Fulton died in 1815 after he fell into the ice-covered Hudson River.

Fulton's steam frigate, which was christened the Fulton I, was so huge that it dwarfed all the other vessels on the river. In November, it was towed to the Jersey City dry dock where the steam engine was to be installed.

Winter Tragedy

That was the last time Fulton ever saw his warship in the water. In January 1815, he traveled to Trenton, New Jersey, to testify in a hearing over steamboat patent disputes. The court proceedings lasted for three weeks. In mid-February, on his way back to New York, he stopped at the dry dock to check the progress on his steam frigate. When he left a few days later, he found that the river was frozen and ferries were not running. So, he and his lawyer, Thomas Emmett, attempted to cross the river by walking across the ice. Emmett was a big man, and the ice was not thick enough to hold him. He fell into the water and Fulton rescued him, but both men ended up soaked from the freezing-cold water.

As a result of the accident, Fulton developed a serious respiratory infection. He seemed as though he might recover, but on the evening of February 22, he took a turn for the worse. He could hardly breathe and had only a faint pulse, and doctors knew they would not be able to save him. The next day, February 23, 1815, Robert Fulton died at his home in New York.

Fulton's Legacy

News of Fulton's death spread quickly. Printed announcements rimmed with heavy black borders appeared in newspapers, and the New York State legislature declared that its members should wear clothes that signified a state of mourning. Fulton's funeral was held one day after he died. It was attended by many dignitaries, including representatives of national and state governments. Prominent members of society also attended, as did common citizens who wanted to honor Fulton one last time. Shops and businesses were closed as a sign of respect, and guns were fired from ships that were docked in the harbor. Fulton was buried in the Livingston family vault in New York City.

Robert Fulton was a highly intelligent, talented, and creative man who was never intimidated by facing new challenges. In many ways, the more difficult the challenge, the more determined he was to conquer it. In his fifty years, he had made enemies as well as friends, and people did not always agree with his methods of going after what he wanted. Yet, from his roots as an impoverished Pennsylvania farm boy with very little formal schooling, Fulton rose to become one of the most successful inventors and entrepreneurs of all time. The steamboat was not his creation alone—but it is his name that is most often associated with it. Robert Fulton was the first person to ever make steamboat transportation a reality. Because of that, he left his mark of genius on the world.

IMPORTANT DATES

1765   Robert Fulton is born in Little Britain Township, Pennsylvania.

1774   Father Robert Fulton Sr. dies.

1776   American David Bushnell designs and builds a submarine called the *American Turtle*.

1783   Claude-François-Dorothée Jouffroy d'Abbans designs a steamboat and launches it on the River Saône in France; the launch is unsuccessful.

1785   Fulton opens his own shop in Philadelphia to specialize in painting miniatures.

1787   Fulton moves to England to study art.

1790   American John Fitch designs and builds steamboat, but it travels so slowly that his endeavor is unsuccessful and he abandons it.

1791   Fulton's paintings are accepted by London's prestigious Royal Academy.

1793   War breaks out between France and England.

1794   Fulton's marble-cutting machine earns silver medal from London's Royal Society for the Encouragement of Arts, Manufacture, and Commerce. Fulton designs a machine to dig canals and is granted a patent for his double-inclined plane.

1796   Fulton writes *A Treatise on the Improvement of Canal Navigation*.

1797   Fulton moves to France. He designs a submarine called the *Nautulus* (spelling later changed to *Nautilus*).

1799   Fulton is granted a French patent for his panorama and he supervises the creation of the first panorama in Paris. Fulton designs a rope-making machine and is granted a French patent for the device.

1800	Fulton demonstrates the *Nautilus* on the River Seine.
1802	Fulton forms a partnership with Robert Livingston, in which they agree to build a steamboat that will operate on the Hudson River in New York.
1803	Fulton's steamboat demonstration on the Seine is successful; Fulton is hailed as "celebrated mechanic."
1804	Fulton accepts an offer to build submarines for the British government and moves back to England.
1806	Fulton's deal with the British falls through; he accepts a financial settlement from British officials and decides to return to America.
1807	Maiden voyage of the steamboat *North River* takes place. Fulton proposes to Harriet Livingston.
1808	Fulton and Harriet Livingston marry in January; son Robert Barlow is born in October.
1810	Fulton publishes a booklet entitled *Torpedo War and Submarine Explosions* to sell torpedo ideas to the American government and naval officials.
1811	The Fulton/Livingston fleet continues to grow as more boats are added. Fulton's daughter Julia is born.
1812	The United States declares war on Great Britain and the War of 1812 begins. Daughter Cornelia is born.
1813	Fulton constructs nation's first dry dock in Jersey City, New Jersey. Robert Livingston and Joel Barlow die. Fulton's fourth child, Mary, is born.
1814	A steam frigate designed by Fulton is demonstrated to American officials, and Congress agrees to finance construction. The demonstration draws thousands of spectators.
1815	Fulton dies and is buried in the Livingston family vault in New York City.

GLOSSARY

Aqueduct: A pipe or channel that is designed to transport water.

Canal: An artificial waterway used for transportation purposes.

Cordelier: A machine for making rope.

Dry dock: A dock that can be kept dry for use when constructing or repairing ships.

Hull: The main frame or body of a ship or boat.

Locks: Enclosures, with gates at each end, that are used to raise or lower boats as they pass from level to level in a canal.

Miniatures: Tiny portraits of people, usually painted on ivory or metal.

Panorama: Huge landscape paintings, usually displayed on buildings or in public settings.

Patent: An exclusive right, granted by the government, to manufacture and sell a product.

Schooner: A two-masted sailboat.

Seine: A river in France that flows through Paris.

Sloop: A one-masted sailboat.

FOR MORE INFORMATION

BOOKS

James M. Flammang, *Robert Fulton: Inventor and Steamboat Builder.* Berkeley Heights, NJ: Enslow, 1999. A book about Fulton's life, work, and achievements.

Alice Crary Sutcliffe, *Robert Fulton and the "Clermont."* New York: Century, 1909. Written by Fulton's great-granddaughter, this book covers Fulton's life, experiments, and many accomplishments.

WEBSITES

Hudson River Maritime Museum
www.ulster.net/~hrmm.
Includes historical details, links to the complete text of several e-books about Robert Fulton, and interesting facts about the history of the steam engine and steamboats.

University of Rochester History Resources —Steam Engine Library
www.history.rochester.edu
A collection of historical documents relating to the steam engine.

Virtualology Museum of History: Robert Fulton
www.robertfulton.org
Site includes much information about Robert Fulton, including an overview of his life and accomplishments. Also, there is an extensive list of links to other sites about Fulton.

SOURCES

1. Alice Crary Sutcliffe, *Robert Fulton and The "Clermont."* New York: Century, 1909, p. 208.

2. Quoted in Sutcliffe, *Robert Fulton and The "Clermont,"* pp. 234–235.

3. Cynthia Owen Philip, Robert Fulton, a Biography. New York: Franklin Watts, 1985, p. 6.

4. Quoted in Sutcliffe, *Robert Fulton and The "Clermont,"* p. 17.

5. Quoted in Sutcliffe, *Robert Fulton and The "Clermont,"* p. 14.

6. Sutcliffe, *Robert Fulton and The "Clermont,"* p. 45.

7. *Transactions*, vol. 12. London: Royal Society for the Encouragement of Arts, Manufactures and Commerce, 1794, p. 329 and 334.

8. Quoted in Kirkpatrick Sale, *The Fire of His Genius: Robert Fulton and the American Dream.* New York: Free Press, 2001, p. 53.

9. Philip, *Robert Fulton, a Biography,* p. 47.

10. Quoted in Philip, *Robert Fulton, a Biography,* p. 54.

11. Quoted in Philip, *Robert Fulton, a Biography,* pp. 72–73.

12. Quoted in Philip, *Robert Fulton, a Biography,* p. 82.

13. Quoted in H.W. Dickinson, *Robert Fulton: Engineer and Artist.* London, 1913. www.history.rochester.edu.

14. Quoted in Philip, *Robert Fulton, a Biography,* p. 89.

15. Quoted in Philip, *Robert Fulton, a Biography,* p. 90.

16. Quoted in Dickinson, *Robert Fulton: Engineer and Artist.*

17. Quoted in Dickinson, *Robert Fulton: Engineer and Artist.*

18. Quoted in Dickinson, *Robert Fulton: Engineer and Artist.*

19. Quoted in Philip, *Robert Fulton, a Biography,* p. 145.

20. Quoted in Sutcliffe, *Robert Fulton and The "Clermont,"* p. 149.

21. Quoted in Sutcliffe, *Robert Fulton and The "Clermont,"* pp. 212–213.

22. Quoted in Philip, *Robert Fulton, a Biography,* p. 283.

23. Quoted in Sale, *The Fire of His Genius,* p. 143.

24. Quoted in Sale, *The Fire of His Genius,* p. 147.

25. Quoted in Philip, *Robert Fulton, a Biography,* p. 328.

INDEX

Albany, 6, 51, 53
Ambinavigator, 20
Aqueducts, 23

Barlow, Ruth and
Joel, 25, 42, 56
Bonaparte, Napoléon,
29, 31, 41
Boulton, Matthew, 20,
45, 46, 49
Bridges, 23
Bushnell, David, 28

Canals, 17–19, 23, 24
digging, 20-3
Cartwright, Edmund,
26, 27, 36–37
Courtenay, William,
16

Double-inclined
plane, 17–19
Drydock, 56, 58

Emmett, Thomas, 59
England, 13–16,
47–48

Ferries, 57
Fishing boat, 11
Franklin, Benjamin,
13, 14
Free trade, 26–27
Frigate, 57–58
Fulton, Robert
as author, 23–24
and canals, 17–19
death of, 59
early life of, 7–13
in England, 13–16,
47–48
family, 7–9, 13,
52–53, 54–55, 57

and inventions,
9–10, 12, 17,
legacy of, 59
as painter, 12–13,
16
in Paris, 25–26,
34–35, 45-46
and steamboats,
42–47
and submarines,
27–31
and war, 26–27
"Fulton's Folly," 6

Guns, 12

Hair-working, 12–13
Hudson River, 4, 53

Inclined plane,
17–19, 23
Inventions, 9-10, 12,
17, 23

Jewelry making,
12-13

Livingston, Harriet,
52–53
Livingston, Robert,
42, 44–46, 49, 52, 56
Locks, 18

Marble, 17
Miniature painting,
13
Mississippi River, 54

Nautilus, 29, 31,
37–41, 47
New York City, 4, 6,
49, 54
North River, 6, 51, 53

Paddlewheels, 4, 11,
51
Painting, 12–13, 16
Panorama, 34–35
Paragon, 54
Paris, 25–26, 34–35,
45-46
Pencil, 9
Philadelphia, 12–13

Rope, 36–37
Royal Academy of
Arts, 15, 16

Seine River, 39, 45, 46
Stanhope, Earl of,
18–19, 20, 24
Steam engine, 4,
19–20, 26, 45, 46,
49
Steam frigate, 57–58
Steamboat, 42–47,
49–51
commercial
operations, 52–55
Submarines, 27–33,
37–41, 47

Torpedoes, 27, 28,
47–49, 55–56
Tuberculosis, 13

War, 26–27, 56
Warm Springs, VA,
13
Warship, 27, 57–58
Watt, James, 20, 45,
46, 49
Weapons, 55–56
West, Benjamin,
14–16